# Animal F

# The Ultimate Audio

# Revision Guide

## By

## Emily Bird

## And

## Jeff Thomas

# Napoleon

I'll rewrite history,
Make it my own story.
I'll rewrite the rules,
Make the others into fools.

**Rule number one**, concerning our foes,
Snowball's a traitor, everyone knows.
He smashed the windmill, and he had aid!
I'll purge his spies, be very afraid.

**Rule number two**, concerning our friends,
To trade with people pays dividends.
So don't assume that two legs are bad,
Selling eggs to men should make you feel glad.

**Rule number three**, concerning clothes,
Pigs can dress up, is what I propose.
We can wear ribbons, medals and hats,
As we become Tsar-like autocrats.

**Rule number four**, concerning beds,
Pigs deserve to rest weary heads.
It's all for you, that we do our best,
Please don't begrudge us a little rest.

**Rule number five**, concerning beer,
It's just for pigs, now get that clear.
Rely on me, your glorious leader,
Portrait and poem, prove I'm your saviour.

**Rule number six**, concerning life,
Death comes to those who cause me strife.
If I see that there is a just cause,
My dogs will kill you with teeth and claws.

*We wrote some rules but
they've been and gone*

*Now here is the law according
to Napoleon*

**The Golden Rule**, above all else,
All beasts are equal, except myself.
Me! I come before all the rest,
I am supreme, I am the best.

# Napoleon

**Vocabulary:** brutal, calculating, corrupt, greedy, patient, perfidious, ruthless, selfish, treacherous, vain.

Napoleon breaks every single rule of Animalism. Complete the table to revise when and how he disobeys the commandments.

| Commandment | Evidence | Effect |
|---|---|---|
| 1. Whatever ... | | |
| 2. Whatever ... | | |
| 3. No animal ... | | |
| 4. No animal ... | | |
| 5. No animal ... | | |
| 6. No animal ... | | |
| 7. All animals ... | | |

# Boxer

*Boxer, dear Boxer, beloved friend,*
*Devoted and loyal until the end.*
*Boxer, dear Boxer, simplest of beasts,*
*Should have questioned your own beliefs.*

A gentle horse, both sweet and good,
Always helped others when he could.
Loved by all, he inspired us,
To work hard, and not make a fuss.

When new rules said clothes were banned,
Sacrificed his hat at this command.
Even though it brought him comfort,
Wanted to prove he was stalwart.

Mighty soldier in the battles,
Main defender during troubles.
Upset when he thought he'd killed,
Soft at heart, it left him chilled.

Couldn't learn past the letter D,
Trusted pigs, and followed blindly.
Napoleon was always right,
Just followed orders didn't fight.

Loyal to Animalism's call,
His mighty strength, admired by all.
Keen to see the windmill complete,
Worked himself near death in this feat.

Looked forward to retirement days,
With Benjamin he'd rest and graze.
But the pigs had an evil plan,
Drove him off in the knacker's van.

# Boxer

**Vocabulary:** brave, dedicated, enthusiastic, honourable, humble, loveable, loyal, obedient, selfless, tender.

Boxer makes many sacrifices throughout the novel. Find quotes to revise all the sacrifices he makes.

| Sacrifice | Quote |
|---|---|
| He burns his straw hat. | |
| He starts to get up 30 minutes earlier than everyone else. | |
| He fights during the Battle of the Cowshed even though he doesn't want to kill any humans. | |
| Boxer contributes the most during the building of the windmill. | |
| He starts to get up 45 minutes earlier than everyone else. | |
| He uses his spare time to carry on working on the windmill. | |
| He starts to get up 60 minutes earlier than everyone else. | |
| Boxer takes a leading role in the Battle of the Windmill. | |
| He continues to work even though he is wounded. | |
| Boxer's lungs collapse as he is working on the windmill. | |

# Two Legs

*Oh Whymper, we've seen you creeping around,*
*Always there if profit is to be found.*

Tsar Nicholas is embodied by Jones,
Too drunk to hear his beast hungry moans.
A failed lawsuit has led you to drink,
Your men are bone idle, don't care what you think..

For days in a row, your animals starve,
Then chased from your farm, it's what you deserve.
Months later on, try and capture it back,
But get knocked in dung, in the attack.

Frederick is symbolic of Hitler,
He cheats the pigs when he buys the timber.
With some fake notes, he pays for the lumber,
To animal-kind there's nobody crueler.

The very next day, you enter the farm,
Blow up the windmill and cause lots of harm.
Once there was the Nazi-Soviet pact,
But friends no more, after this warlike act.

Pilkington is the Capitalist West,
Fears Animalism will spread unrest.
Thought he'd made allies with lumber trade,
Said 'serves you right' when the pigs were betrayed.

An uneasy peace, then seems to arise,
But two aces are played, still both full of lies.
Tension in Tehran, Yalta and Potsdam,
Grew more and more as the Cold War began.

### Two legs bad!

# Two legs

**Vocabulary:** aggressive, cruel, lazy, dishonest, fraudulent, grasping, hard-hearted, irresponsible, negligent, violent.

Complete the table in order to revise all the bad qualities exhibited by the humans. Explain how these qualities make the reader feel.

| Quality/character | Evidence | Explain |
|---|---|---|
| Aggressive/Frederick | | |
| Cruel/Jones | | |
| Lazy/Jones' men | | |
| Dishonest/Pilkington | | |
| Fraudulent/Frederick | | |
| Grasping/Whymper | | |
| Hard-hearted/knacker's van driver | | |
| Irresponsible/Jones | | |
| Selfish/Jones | | |
| Violent/Frederick | | |

# Snowball

*The dreams I had, just yesterday,*
*Are gone for good, melted away.*
*Not a snowball's chance in hell,*
*In this Soviet parallel.*

Thought I was a clever leader,
Read those books to make life better.
I wrote the farm's name on the gate,
And tried to make you literate.

Though I was a model leader,
Honoured our first ovine martyr.
Clung to ideals of Major's dream,
Avid fan of the Marxist scheme.

Though I was a warlike leader,
Tactics from campaigns of Caesar.
Helped defeat invading humans,
Won a medal for brave actions.

Thought I was the favoured leader,
In debates a great orator.
Did not become corrupt like some,
But extra milk was most welcome.

Though I was an astute leader,
Spread the message to our neighbour.
Worldwide move to revolution,
Make friends not foes was my solution.

But I was a foolish scapegoat,
Napoleon was so cutthroat.
Purged me from the model farm,
And blamed me for all future harm.

# Snowball

**Vocabulary:** ardent, fervent, idealistic, inattentive, ingenuous, intelligent, naive, scapegoat, thoughtful.

Each and every one of Snowball's dreams is destroyed, explain why each dream fails and find quotes to support your comments.

| Dream | Why it fails | Quote |
|---|---|---|
| To follow in Old Major's dream and ensure equality for all animals. | | |
| To enable all animals to become literate, so that they are all equal. | | |
| To run an egg laying committee, so that all fowl feel supported. | | |
| To run a hygiene committee, so that all cows are comfortable. | | |
| To run a committee for the wild animals so they can join in with Animalism. | | |
| To run a wool committee so all sheep feel included in Animalism. | | |
| To build a windmill so that it can provide energy to make life easier. | | |

# Four Legs

Muriel the goat, reads the news,
Yesterday's papers, futile views.

Clover the horse, so motherly,
Comforted all, so lovely.
Tended Boxer, concerned for him,
Stayed by his side when times were grim.

Faithful to Animalism,
Challenged Mollie's egotism.
Sensed the rules were being altered,
But left tongue tied and thoughts faltered.

Benjamin just so cynical,
Said pigs' conduct was typical.
Didn't bother to read or to write,
Nothing in life gave him delight.

Only cared for his friend Boxer,
Loved to graze beside his partner.
At the end you worked out his fate,
But by then it was far too late.

Mollie the pony was so vain,
Just wanted ribbons in her mane.
She found excuses not to toil,
Hid herself during the battle.

Didn't try hard to read or write,
Just wrote her name, a pretty sight.
Couldn't live without her sugar,
Defected to a new owner.

# Four legs

**Vocabulary:** behind, caring, contemptuous, cynical, foolish, ignorant, motherly, passive, supportive, vain.

Use the vocabulary to complete the table about these key four legged characters. Find quotes and then explain how these animals help Orwell to convey his message.

| Four legged character | Quote | Message |
|---|---|---|
| Clover is... | | |
| Clover is... | | |
| Clover is... | | |
| Benjamin is... | | |
| Benjamin is... | | |
| Benjamin is... | | |
| Mollie is... | | |
| Mollie is... | | |
| Mollie is... | | |
| Muriel is... | | |

# Squealer and the dogs

*I can turn black into white,*
*Persuade you that day is night.*
*Pigs' propaganda machine,*
*I'll make you doubt what you've seen.*

Propaganda through use of fear,
Say Farmer Jones is lurking near.
Scare the beasts, make them good and meek,
Keeps us pigs strong and others weak.

Propaganda through use of lies,
Readjustments to food supplies.
Tell them life is better than ever,
Now they have their porcine leader.

Propaganda through emotions,
Tell the beasts of our devotions.
And for their doubts, make them feel guilt,
Say that on trust is this farm built.

Propaganda through documents,
Claim to have proof of true events.
Use these to blacken Snowball's name,
To make him scapegoat is my aim.

Propaganda through distraction,
I'll skip about while they listen.
Frisking movements will bewilder,
Clear arguments I will hinder.

And if you beasts doubt what I say,
Just beware, there'll be hell to pay.
For at my back and always near,
Are vicious dogs that you all fear.

# Squealer and the dogs

**Vocabulary:** articulate, bewildering, eloquent, hostile, immoral, intimidating, menacing, persuasive, threatening.

Revise how Napoleon uses Squealer's propaganda and the dogs' intimidating presence at key events during the novel.

| Key Event | How Squealer/dogs support Napoleon |
|---|---|
| Napoleon announces there will be no more meetings. Chapter 5. | |
| Napoleon decides that the windmill will be constructed after all. Chapter 5. | |
| Napoleon starts to trade with humans. Chapter 6. | |
| Napoleon and the pigs move into the farmhouse and start sleeping in beds. Chapter 6. | |
| Napoleon wants to eliminate the four porkers. Chapter 7. | |
| Napoleon changes the farm's anthem. Chapter 7. | |
| Napoleon wants to develop a cult status. Chapters 7 and 8. | |
| Napoleon wants to start brewing and drinking alcohol. Chapter 8. | |
| Napoleon wants to reduce the animals' rations. Chapter 9. | |

# Structure of Animal Farm

## Chronological plan,
## Fable links beast and man.

At the start, life's not fair,
Farmer Jones does not care.
Makes you feel the beasts' plight,
Hope they will rise and fight.

Wise old pig, shares his dream,
Overthrow old regime.
Rousing words set the tone,
Seeds of change, quickly sown.

Moses flees when Jones leaves,
Faith is gone, he perceives.
He comes back, at the end,
New regime, is his friend.

No flashbacks in this prose,
Step by step, pigs' greed grows.
'til they are, just like men,
Manor Farm, named again.

Cyclical, structuring,
Orwell is predicting,
Not the first, not the last,
These events come to pass.

Noble rules are phased out,
Pigs in charge, there's no doubt.
Fairy tale, not found here,
Happy end, nowhere near.

# Structure

**Vocabulary:** chronological, consecutive, cumulative, cyclical, linear, repetition, reoccurring, sequential.

Orwell structures the novel so that the pigs' corruption grows step by step. Revise how their corruption grows.

| Corruption | Quote | Effect on other animals |
|---|---|---|
| Napoleon drinks all the milk on the first day. | | |
| The pigs continue to keep all the milk for themselves. | | |
| The pigs don't do any physical work. | | |
| The pigs keep all the apples for themselves. | | |
| The pigs start to trade with humans. | | |
| The pigs move into the farmhouse. | | |
| The pigs get up later than all the others. | | |
| Napoleon awards himself medals. | | |
| Napoleon has the four porkers executed. | | |
| The gun has to be fired on Napoleon's birthday. | | |
| The pigs start drinking alcohol. | | |
| Napoleon builds a school for his piglets. | | |
| Napoleon is elected unanimously. | | |
| Napoleon changes the name of the farm. | | |

# Themes in Animal Farm

*Foolish dreams,*
*Power schemes,*
*Are key themes.*

Old Major's dream begins the tale,
Snowball hopes schemes will prevail.
Boxer yearns to build the windmill,
But these dreams amount to nil.

Mollie's foolish with her ribbons,
While others should ask more questions.
With fake notes, Napoleon's fooled,
The sheep don't know they're being ruled.

Animals suffer under man,
But fare worse in pigs' plan.
Many hurt in mans' attacks,
Toil against windmill setbacks.

Jones has the power then loses it,
Napoleon rules as he sees fit.
Beasts with brains take all the power,
Beasts with brawn are made to cower.

Equal under communism,
And the same for Animalism.
But men and pigs corrupt ideals,
Change the rules with their repeals.

Class should be banished in the past,
But its power seems to last.
Beasts fall into their set roles,
Is inequality in our souls?

# Themes

**Vocabulary:** class, control, corruption, dreams, education, equality, foolishness, hopes, pride, violence.

This novel has many interwoven themes. Find as much evidence as possible for each theme and make a note of the characters involved.

| Theme | Evidence | Characters |
|---|---|---|
| Class | | |
| Control | | |
| Corruption | | |
| Dreams | | |
| Education | | |
| Equality | | |
| Foolishness | | |
| Hopes | | |
| Pride | | |
| Violence | | |

# Language in Animal Farm

*Allegorical and symbolic,*

*Accessible and metaphoric.*

Fairy tale is ironic,
As the ending is so tragic.
The language is so satiric,
Its bitter tone is acerbic.

Visions led to an uprising,
Major's words were mesmerising.
But words also make illusion,
Sugarcandy's a delusion.

Animals silenced, meetings banned,
With no voice you can't make a stand.
When porkers spoke up they were killed,
Their massacre left others chilled.

Anthems inspired unity,
Their first song gave identity.
Anthems then lead to misery,
Second song brought despondency.

Constant slogans and sheep bleatings,
To interrupt Snowball's meetings.
I must work harder Boxer says,
Keep him going 'til dying days.

Lying, is used to justify,
Pigs use it as their alibi.
And Snowball's name is vilified,
Pigs claim that he cheated and spied.

# The language

**Vocabulary:** caveats, lies, literacy, maxims, propaganda, rhetorical questions, rules, silence, slogans.

The language of the novel is very straightforward. Explore the effects of this understated language style at key moments.

| Key Moment | Effect of the language |
|---|---|
| **Chapter 1** Jones is an irresponsible farmer. | |
| **Chapter 2** The animals can stand their hunger no longer. | The straightforward language emphasizes the animal's physical need and shows that they are desperate, not malicious or hysterical. |
| **Chapter 3** The pigs are 'supervising' the farm work. | |
| **Chapter 4** The cat puts her claws into an invading human's neck. | |
| **Chapter 5** None of the animals ever speak of Mollie once she leaves. | |
| **Chapter 6** The workload increases. | |
| **Chapter 7** Three dogs attack Boxer. | |
| **Chapter 8** Pinkeye the pig becomes Napoleon's official food taster. | |
| **Chapter 9** Napoleon has fathered lots of piglets. | |
| **Chapter 10** The sheep start saying two legs are better. | |

# Historical Context

*Remember it's an allegory,*
*Not just straightforward history.*

Revolt against the hated Tsar,
Lenin becomes head Commissar.
Revolt against the hated Jones,
The beasts take over all he owns.

Put on show is Lenin's body,
Stalin's proof that they were friendly.
Put on show is Major's relic,
Napoleon is now his mimic.

Fighting for control of Moscow,
In civil war, Reds beat White foe.
Fighting for control of farmstead,
Beasts win Battle of the Cowshed.

Leadership contest now begins,
Trotsky's banished and Stalin wins.
Leadership contest now begins,
Snowball flees, Napoleon wins.

Men forced to give up their harvest,
If they refused they faced arrest.
Hens forced to give up their produce,
Collectivisation is abuse.

Building projects, five year plans,
Men died constructing roads and dams.
Building projects, windmill scheme,
Mirrors Stalin's industrial dream.

# Historical Context

**Vocabulary:** allegory, Bolsheviks, collectivisation, Communism, Five-Year-Plans, show-trials, Stalin, purges.

**Use the vocabulary to complete the following cloze exercise in order to revise the historical context of *Animal Farm*.**

*Animal Farm* is an _____ of the 1917 Russian Revolution. In the October of 1917 the _____ took control of Russia. The Bolshevik Party believed in a political ideal called _____ where everyone should live in equality.

In 1924, Lenin, the leader of the Bolsheviks died, and a bitter power struggle ensued between two main contenders: _____ and Trotsky.

Through a series of schemes, Stalin took power. One of Stalin's key policies was that of _____, which was supposedly aimed at modernising Russia's agricultural system. In reality, it just gave Stalin's government direct control over agricultural produce. They used the produce to feed the growing urban population, as well as exporting some of it to foreign countries. The produce was forcibly taken and the result was that millions in the countryside died from famine.

Stalin also introduce a series of _____, which were intended to improve Russia's industrial output and infrastructure. In reality, millions of people died under the harsh working conditions demanded by these schemes.

In order to maintain control, Stalin instigated a series of _____, in which key Communist party members were put through _____ and then executed, in order to remove anyone who might pose a threat to his leadership.

Try getting your friends and family involved in your revision so that you can try out some of these drama based revision activities...

- Mime all the animals gathering at the start to hear Old Major's speech. Try to portray your animal's personality through your movement and where you choose to sit. *What do you learn about the dynamics on the farm at the start of the novel?*

- Improvise a scene where Moses the raven talks about Sugarcandy Mountain. How does he describe this place? What questions do the other animals ask him about it? *What does this tell you about the animals' needs and dreams?*

- Arrange freeze-frames for key moments in the Battle of the Cowshed. How do the animals defend their new farm? *What can you learn about the animals' attitudes towards the humans?*

- Stage a debate between Napoleon and Snowball, where Napoleon argues that the animals need to concentrate on food production, while Snowball tries to persuade others that the windmill is what they should be working on. Remember to stay in character, Napoleon's speeches are always short and to the point, where as Snowball is more persuasive. *What do you learn about the characters here?*

- Perform a slow-motion version of the humans putting the blasting powder under the windmill. What might the key animals do at this point? *What does this tell you about the theme of responsibility?*

- Re-enact the scene where Boxer collapses and Clover tends him. What do they say to each other? *What hopes do these two horses have for the future?*

- Devise a scene where the pigs negotiate with Alfred Simmonds the owner of the knacker's yard about taking Boxer away. What deal do they make? Do they intend to get rid of other animals this way in the future? *What do you learn about the depth of the pigs' greed and corruption?*

- Hot seat Napoleon and have him questioned by other farmers, in order to find out how he's managed to make Animal Farm so efficient. *What do you learn about the attitudes of both the farmers and Napoleon?*

# Useful exam tips... a few pointers that might help:

- Work smarter not harder: listen to the guide as often as possible, for example when walking to school or doing your paper round. This is dead time that can be used effectively to really get to know the facts.

- Get someone to test you on the quizzes.

- Know which exam board and which texts you are using. I know this sounds obvious, but exams sometimes have lots of different option choices in one paper. Only do the questions on the texts you have studied for.

- Never waffle. Just answer the question. Don't assume more writing equals more marks.

- Look at as many past papers as possible before the big day. Get to know the style of questions you are likely to be asked.

- Download our model answers and read over them several times, to really get to know them.

- Practice writing your own responses to these questions and then compare.

- Use the exam board mark schemes and grade the model essays to see where they've met the requirements.

- If at first you feel you don't know the answer to a question, leave it and come back to it. Build your confidence by answering the questions you know well first. Remember you can answer the questions in any order.

- Learn your key words, as spelling is important.

# About us...

**Emily Bird** has been an English teacher for over twelve years and an AQA examiner for four years. She is a full time teacher and a specialist in teaching dyslexic pupils. When she's not working on Revision Rocks material you will find her reading novels and writing fiction.

**Jeff Thomas** has been a History teacher for over a decade and currently teaches at Worthing College. He lives in probably the coolest place in England: Brighton.

Jeff has appeared on: BBC 5 Live, BBC Sussex, Kent, London and Surrey to talk about cutting edge revision techniques and Revision Rocks. Jeff has been featured in the Times Educational Supplement (TES) on two occasions, in relation to revising through song. Jeff has also made many radio appearances for the BBC, to discuss issues relating to history and secondary education, which he says makes him feel very important within the world of history teaching.

Customer satisfaction guaranteed: We want you to be entirely happy with our products. If for any reason there is a problem, please contact us directly: jeff.thomas@revisionrocks.co.uk and we promise to solve the issue.

## All Revision Guides are equal,

## but some are more equal than others